Rose

A Comedy

by

Andrew Davies

No part of this book may be reproduced, stored in a retrieval system, or transmitted in any form, by any means, including mechanical, electronic, photocopying, recording, or otherwise, without the prior written permission of the publisher.

SAMUEL FRENCH, INC.
25 WEST 45TH STREET   NEW YORK 10036
7623 SUNSET BOULEVARD   HOLLYWOOD 90046
LONDON   *TORONTO*

Copyright ©, 1980, by Andrew Davies

ALL RIGHTS RESERVED

CAUTION: Professionals and amateurs are hereby warned that ROSE is subject to a royalty. It is fully protected under the copyright laws of the United States of America, the British Commonwealth, including Canada, and all other countries of the Copyright Union. All rights, including professional, amateur, motion pictures, recitation, lecturing, public reading, radio broadcasting, television, and the rights of translation into foreign languages are strictly reserved. In its present form the play is dedicated to the reading public only.

ROSE may be given stage presentation by amateurs upon payment of a royalty of Fifty Dollars for the first performance, and Forty Dollars for each additional performance, payable one week before the date when the play is given to Samuel French, Inc., at 25 West 45th Street, New York, N.Y. 10036, or at 7623 Sunset Boulevard, Hollywood, Calif. 90046, or to Samuel French (Canada), Ltd., 80 Richmond Street East, Toronto, Ontario, Canada M5C 1P1.

Royalty of the required amount must be paid whether the play is presented for charity or gain and whether or not admission is charged.

Stock royalty quoted on application to Samuel French, Inc.

For all other rights than those stipulated above, apply to Gilbert Parker, c/o William Morris Agency, Inc., 1350 Avenue of the Americas, NYC 10019.

Particular emphasis is laid on the question of amateur or professional readings, permission and terms for which must be secured in writing from Samuel French, Inc.

Copying from this book in whole or in part is strictly forbidden by law, and the right of performance is not transferable.

Whenever the play is produced the following notice must appear on all programs, printing and advertising for the play: "Produced by special arrangement with Samuel French, Inc."

Due authorship credit must be given on all programs, printing and advertising for the play.

Anyone presenting the play shall not commit or authorize any act or omission by which the copyright of the play or the right to copyright same may be impaired.

No changes shall be made in the play for the purpose of your production unless authorized in writing.

The publication of this play does not imply that it is necessarily available for performance by amateurs or professionals. Amateurs and professionals considering a production are strongly advised in their own interests to apply to Samuel French, Inc., for consent before starting rehearsals, advertising, or booking a theatre or hall.

Printed in U.S.A.

ISBN 0 573 61507 1

SOUNDTRACK ROSE

ACT I

Opening–		Instrumental "Sound of Silence" Noisy children in background
P.	Slops–	Bar Noise
P.	Assembly–	Piano - "Jesus Loves Me"– Children's voices singing
P.	Sc. change–	Noisy children over scene change

ACT II

P.	Bedroom–	(flashback) explosion of gas water heater *may not be use but to be available during previews just in case
P.		repeat of "Sound of Silence"
P.	Slops–	Bar noise Car noise
P.	Sc change–	Children in playground over scene change
P.		Opening verse "All Things Bright and Beautiful"

DUKE OF YORK'S THEATRE
ST MARTIN'S LANE, LONDON, WC2H 0DH

SOLE PROPRIETOR & LICENSEE: THE DUKE OF YORK'S THEATRE LTD.

COLIN BROUGH
for The Lupton Theatre Company Ltd presents

GLENDA JACKSON

in

ROSE

a new play by
ANDREW DAVIES

with

STEPHANIE COLE DAVID DAKER DIANA DAVIES TOM GEORGESON
JEAN HEYWOOD GILLIAN MARTELL RICHARD VANSTONE

Directed by
ALAN DOSSOR

Lighting by   Designed by   Costumes by
ANDY PHILLIPS   JOHN GUNTER   LINDY HEMMING

First performance at The Duke Of York's Theatre, Thursday 28th February 1980

Characters in order of appearance

Rose	GLENDA JACKSON
Mother	JEAN HEYWOOD
Smale	STEPHANIE COLE
Malpass	GILLIAN MARTELL
Jim Beam	TOM GEORGESON
Sally	DIANA DAVIES
Jake	RICHARD VANSTONE
Geoffrey	DAVID DAKER
Father	RICHARD VANSTONE

The play takes place in and around a Midlands town

OPENING NIGHT, MARCH 26, 1981

CORT THEATRE

Ⓢ A Shubert Organization Theatre

Gerald Schoenfeld, *Chairman* — Bernard B. Jacobs, *President*

Elizabeth I. McCann Nelle Nugent
The Shubert Organization
in association with
Colin Brough for The Lupton Theatre Company, Ltd.
and Warner Theatre Productions Inc.

present

Glenda Jackson

in

ROSE

also starring

Jessica Tandy

by **Andrew Davies**

with

Guy Boyd   John Cunningham   Jo Henderson
Margaret Hilton   Beverly May   J.T. Walsh
Lori Cardille   Cynthia Crumlish   Don McAllen Leslie

| Setting by | Costumes by | Lighting by |
| John Gunter | Linda Fisher | Andy Phillips |

Set Supervision by Tom Lynch

Directed by
Alan Dossor

"Rose" was originally produced in London by
Colin Brough for The Lupton Theatre Company, Ltd.

The Producers and Theatre Management are Members
of The League of New York Theatres and Producers, Inc.

CAST (*in order of appearance*)

Rose	GLENDA JACKSON
Mother	JESSICA TANDY
Smale	BEVERLY MAY
Malpass	MARGARET HILTON
Jim Beam	J. T. WALSH
Sally	JO HENDERSON
Jake	GUY BOYD
Geoffrey	JOHN CUNNINGHAM
School Caretaker and Teachers	DON MCALLEN LESLIE, CYNTHIA CRUMLISH, LORI CARDILLE

"Rose" takes place in and around a Midlands town.

CHARACTERS

ROSE
MOTHER (north eastern accent I think)
SMALE, a headmistress
MALPASS, a teacher
JIM BEAM, the primary adviser
SALLY
JAKE
GEOFFREY, Rose's husband
FATHER, only heard

The action takes place in and around a Midlands Town.

Rose

ACT I

SLOPS WINE BAR

At curtain rise we see ROSE *seated at a table smoking a cigarette: nothing much else is visible. On the table is a half of bitter and a sherry. In the backround we hear "The Sounds of Silence". As the lights come up behind the ten doors around the set we hear:*

SMALE. Mrs. Malpass will tell the story. Fingers on lips.

MALPASS. Once upon a time there was girl who thought she was very clever.

BRAM. I'm just looking for some kind of spark, you know? I think you might have got it.

MOTHER. You must be fond of a treat, turning out on a night like this.

SALLY. Warwickshire's a lovely county, Rose, it's just the people who live here.

GEOFFREY. Do you know, there's not so much as a piece of bloody cheese in the house.

JAKE. Susan.

GEOFFREY. It doesn't matter.

JAKE. No. . .

(*Abruptly: the music fades, the lights behind the doors go out, the lights in the central playing area come up full and in the backround we hear bar sounds.*)

(MOTHER *enters and crosses in to table.*)

MOTHER. Well, that was a nasty experience, Rose. And the lock wouldn't work.

ROSE. Did you get invaded then?

MOTHER. I'd like to see them try.

ROSE. Well never mind, you'll be all right at the theatre, Mother they've got quite a nice toilet there.

MOTHER. I'll beg leave to doubt *that*, Rose. Seemed a pokey little place to me. And that lad in the ticket office. Selling tickets in his T-shirt, there's no need for that!

ROSE. Well, it's only the *studio* theatre, Mother.

MOTHER. They used to do that in evening suits. That lad at the ballet had one.

ROSE. Who?

MOTHER. That time you took me to the ballet.

ROSE. Which time?

MOTHER. That time we went to the ballet. The *only* time! When we went to the *big* theatre, the *proper* theatre! Don't you remember Rose, we were sat there, waiting, and then a man came on in evening dress with a piece of paper. . .

ROSE. Oh, yes.

MOTHER. And then he said that owing to an indisposition Serge somebody would not be able to dance the part of the Prince, and everyone in the whole theatre moaned. Yes, a great moan went up. It's funny, I didn't know who this Serge was from Adam, I'd never seen him in my life before, but I felt I had to join in that moan. (*Pause.*) I enjoyed that moment more than anything else in the whole evening.

ROSE. You would.

MOTHER. (*Sharply.*) What?

ROSE. Nothing.

MOTHER. You didn't have to ask me out tonight, you know.

ROSE. I *wanted* to.

MOTHER. Can't think why.

ROSE. Oh, mother. (*Pause.*)

MOTHER. That's the only evening suit I've set eyes on all the time I've been down here.

ROSE. Well, they don't wear them so much nowadays.

MOTHER. You don't need to tell me that, Rose, that's what I'm saying. No danger of finding one in this place, is there? What do they call it?

ROSE. Slops Wine Bar, mother.

MOTHER. Yes. I know what sort of place this is.

ROSE. What?

MOTHER. (*With deep contempt.*) *Casual.*

ROSE. Oh, dear.

MOTHER. There's no need to make fun of me, Rose, you know what I'm talking about. Look at that one behind the bar, I'd like to know what *his* aim is, shirt open down to there. And earrings. *That's* not necessary, Rose.

ROSE. He's only got one earring, mother.

MOTHER. Don't know what he's so proud of, he's as hairy as a monkey.

ROSE. Mother!

MOTHER. And he's got a belly like a poisoned pup.

ROSE. Ssh!

MOTHER. No need to shush me, they don't care one way or the other, people like that.

ROSE. Oh, mother, how d'you *know*?

MOTHER. Well, it's obvious, Rose.

ROSE. Oh, that's typical.

MOTHER. I didn't ask to come here tonight, I know you didn't want to bring me.

ROSE. I did, I did, look how many times I asked you.

MOTHER. Oh, asking's one thing.

ROSE. What's that supposed to mean?

MOTHER. I don't want to say any more about it.

ROSE. I wanted you to come out with me, I wanted you to come out with me and have a nice time. I thought we'd enjoy ourselves! I thought it would be nice for you to come out and see somewhere different and have a couple of drinks, instead of being stuck home every night!

MOTHER. There's no need for you to feel sorry for me.

ROSE. (*Loud.*) It's not that!

MOTHER. Ssh!

ROSE. It's not that! Can't you understand it? I thought it would be nice to go out with you for a change! (*They're both cross with each other.*)

MOTHER. What's the matter with your husband?

ROSE. There's nothing the matter with my husband! I wish you wouldn't call him that.

MOTHER. Well, he is that, isn't he?

ROSE. He's got a name, hasn't he?

MOTHER. I know he's got a name, there's no need to talk to me as if I was halfwitted, and where is he anyway?

ROSE. It doesn't matter where he is, he's got nothing to do with this, this was going to be an evening for you and me.

MOTHER. Hm.

ROSE. He's got some *thing* on in Birmingham.

MOTHER. What sort of thing?

ROSE. I don't know. One of his things.

MOTHER. Well, I hope he remembers he's married.

(*She brings this out with some triumph.* ROSE *lets out a big exasperated sigh. Pause. Then, makes an effort.*)

ROSE. Mother! Look. Let's have another drink. We've got time.

MOTHER. No, thank you.

ROSE. Oh, come on.

MOTHER. Not for me, Rose, thank you.

ROSE. I think I will.

MOTHER. I don't need alcohol to enjoy myself. It's no use trying to turn me into an alcoholic.

ROSE. I'm not trying to turn you into an alcoholic, I just thought you might fancy the other half, that's all!

MOTHER. And I don't like to see women drinking beer either.

ROSE. I'll turn the other way.

MOTHER. I'm sorry, I just don't like to see it. Women never used to drink beer.

ROSE. Ah, well, that's emancipation for you, mother. But I only drink halves, don't I? Only halfway there in the struggle for self-realisation. The spirit's willing, honest, it's just the flesh. If it weren't for the dreaded cystitis, I'd drink pint for pint with any man here.

MOTHER. No need for that, Rose.

ROSE. Oh, think of all the things there's no *need* for! If we were all like you no one would ever do *anything*!

MOTHER. Well, I'm sorry I'm spoiling your evening, I can see you won't invite me again in a hurry.

ROSE. Look, for the last time, I *wanted* you to come with me, and I'm sorry if I *asked* and *asked*, but *I don't know* any other way of getting people to do things.

(*A splutter of protest from* MOTHER.)

What did you want me to do, kidnap you? And I just wish you'd stop talking about spoiling my evening and no need for this and no need for that, because I wish you could just get it into your *thick* head that this is supposed to be just you and me going out together and having a nice time just for a change, because you're my *mother* and I *love* you!

MOTHER. If you're going to talk to me like that I'm going now.

ROSE. Like what, for Christ's sake? What do you *want*?

MOTHER. Somebody here might know us!

ROSE. Nobody here knows us! Nobody knows anybody!

MOTHER. Oh, stop trying to be clever, you don't suit it. All right, if you're quite determined that I've got to make an exhibition of myself, I'll tell you! I don't want you worrying about me and feeling guilty about me, and I know it's not for me anyway, it's to make you feel better; and if you think I'm not making an effort and keeping my mind alive, well haven't you ever stopped to think I might not *want* to keep my mind alive! What do I want to keep my mind alive for? I don't need to keep my mind alive! You're like that old woman next door always trying to get me to go and play Bingo with her!

ROSE. Well, why not Bingo?

MOTHER. I'll tell you why not Bingo, because I did go once, which you never have, I went with that woman next door, and we sat and played Bingo, all us old widows, and it might have been all right for them but it wasn't all right for me, he didn't have any colored lights and bouncing balls, he just took numbers out of a box, no pretending there was any fun about it at all, just a lot of old widows trying to take their minds off waiting to die, all those numbers, seventy-nine, eighty-five, it just makes it worse, if you had the wit to see it, which you don't, you just think about yourself, don't you, and whether you've done enough, well have you, you've done quite enough, and you don't have to worry about me any more, thank you very much, and it was very nice of you to ask me out, but you needn't have bothered. You'll see when you come to it yourself, it'll be like the scales falling off your eyes, you'll see. You just want to be let alone, and not mucked about and made to see the point of things. Ooh, it'll be such a relief when I'm dead. Eeh! I'm sorry about that little outburst, I think

I'll take meself home now, you go to the play and enjoy yourself, Rose—

ROSE. Don't be silly. I'll come with you.

MOTHER. No, I'd never forgive myself.

ROSE. Right!

MOTHER. No, I'll get the bus and I'll be home and tucked up in bed by nine and that'll have seen another day off, it's putting the time in that counts. (*Suddenly stands up, produces a pound note, slaps it down.*) Have one for me. (*She walks Off.*)

ROSE. Mother!

MOTHER. And remember you're married. (*She's gone.*)

ROSE. Terrible. Terrible. (*During this next bit she moves from "the scene at the table" to "*ROSE *addressing the Audience" perhaps by way of addressing her first remarks to people at the next table. Well I'm sorry to have inflicted all that on you. (Laughing.*) I mean I do realise that you can perfectly well get all that sort of thing in your own homes, I mean you've all got mothers somewhere, I s'pose. Yes? And my only excuse is this, something Rosa Luxembourg said: that it's in the tiny domestic struggles of individual people as they grope towards self-realisation that we can most truly discern the great movements of society. Splendid, that. It's O.K. I saw it on a Tee-Shirt. Yes, it was a bloody big Tee-Shirt.

ROSE. So I went round next day, and we made it up, no hard feelings, because she is my mother, and I do love her and who else has she got, and we have that sort of scene, if you can believe it, about once every three weeks; and really, if her idea of enjoying herself is having a bad time, who am I to interfere in the twilight of her life? Still, you know all about that. And anyway, this isn't about her, it's about me, she thinks it's about her but it isn't, it's about me. I'm not just a pretty face.

I have a job. Yes, I teach 6 year olds in an infant school, and it's worthwhile and I'm quite ambitious, I fancy becoming some new kind of head mistress. But, oh, if you could see it.

(STOKES *enters briskly.*)

STOKES. (*Sourly.*) Finished with this lot have you?
ROSE. (*Brightly.*) Yes, thank you Mr. Stokes. (*Conspiratorily, to audience.*) School caretaker. He's the only man to be found in the infant school because the teaching staff, you see, is entirely female.

(*Two female teachers enter and exchange good mornings with* ROSE.)

ROSE. (*Perhaps modulating this according to whether* STOKES *is on stage/off stage listening or not to any given bit, because she doesn't want to offend him.*) So Mr. Stokes is the big, strong man who looks after his school and keeps it neat and tidy, and us female teachers, well we're the wayward girls who mess it up for him, and we're expected to say we're so sorry we made all the mess, Mr. Stokes, and thank you *so much*. . . Real education *does* make a mess, and we should not apologize for it. Here's one teacher who isn't going to play that game, today. I am not going to end up saying sorry . . . Sorry! (*She said it involuntarily. She is furious with herself. Could she act that out and then acknowledge the humour.*) Well, schools are like that. How can I explain? Well, let's say it's assembly and I'm late.

THE ASSEMBLY
SMALE, MALPASS and TEACHERS. (*Singing lustily.*)
JESUS LOVES ME,
THIS I KNOW,
FOR THE BIBLE TELLS ME SO

Rose. (*Sneaking on and joining in.*)

SORRY!

All. (*Continued.*)

LITTLE ONES TO HIM BELONG
THEY ARE WEAK BUT HE IS STRONG

YES, JESUS LOVES ME.
YES, JESUS LOVES ME.

YES, JESUS LOVES ME
THE BIBLE TELLS ME SO.

(Smale *has noticed* Rose's *late arrival with disapproval.* Smale's *fierce eyes are everywhere, glaring at imaginary offenders in the Audience.*)

Smale. And now, let me see you all sitting very quietly. Fingers on lips. I'm waiting, (Garth *D.L.*) *Fingers on lips.* Thank you. Now Mrs. Malpass will tell the story, and today the story is called "The Wonderful Box."

(Smale *and* Rose *sit down,* Malpass forward.)

Malpass. Once upon a time there was a little girl called Jane; and she went to school, just like you, but she wasn't a very happy little girl. Because she was very poor, and she didn't have any toys to play with. Every day she'd see the other children playing with their toys: the boys with their footballs and the girls with their dolls. . .

(Rose *might wince.*)

But oh, how Jane wished that she had something of her very own to play with. It was no use asking her mother, because she knew her mother didn't have any money to spare. So she became sadder and sadder. Then one morning, as she was walking to school, suddenly she noticed something in the gutter. What d'you think it was?

(SMALE *leans forward urgently, fingers on lips, lest someone break the silence.*)

It was a little wooden box. It was shiny and carved, with a little golden lock with the key in it, and Jane thought she'd never seen such a beautiful box. She bent down. . . (MALPASS *mimes it.*) and she turned it round in her hands . . . and then she turned the key and opened the lid . . . and what a surprise! Beautiful music came out of the box! It was a musical box! And then she closed the box, and hugged it tight. But then she thought: It's not my box. So she stood there, clutching the box and wondering what to do. And what d'you think she did?

(SMALE *leans forward as before.*)

No! She was a good, honest little girl, although she was so poor, and she did take it to her teacher. And the teacher went with her to the police station, and the policeman said he was very sorry, but a rich little boy had come to the police station in a big shiny car and said he'd lost the box. It belonged to him.

(ROSE *blows out a great breath.*)

So you can imagine how sad Jane was. But the very next day, the same big shiny car drew up outside Jane's house, and out of it got the rich little boy and his daddy, and the daddy had a parcel in his hand. Another box! Almost as beautiful as the one Jane had found. "Open it," said the little rich boy. And very slowly Jane opened it. (MALPASS *mimes.*) And the box played a beautiful tune for Jane. Can you hear the music? I can hear it. (*She cups her hand to her ear.*) Cup your hands to your ears when I open the box.

(*She opens it.* SMALE, *glaring, and* ROSE, *deadpan, cup their hands to their ears simultaneously like a backing group.*)

And then the rich little boy and his daddy got into the big shiny car and drove away. But Jane was very happy, because she had something of her own to play with at last! And it was all because she was a *good*, *honest* little girl who respected other people's property. And if you are all good honest boys and girls—I'm sure you are—who knows? Maybe one day you might have a wonderful box of your own. (*With a demure, smug, almost embryonic curtsey to* SMALE, MALPASS *sits down.*)

SMALE. Hands together. Close eyes. *Tight. Everybody.* Mrs. Fidgett will say the prayer for today.

(ROSE, *alarmed, she'd forgotten it was her turn. She'll have to improvise.*)

ROSE. Oh God.

(*A rather long pause. Her mind's gone blank.* SMALE *and* MALPASS *go very tense.* ROSE *clears throat.*)

Oh God. Help us to make this a happy day at school. Help us to enjoy the maths and the work cards and the apparatus and the music and movement today. Look after us at play time and help us not to get into fights. You know we sometimes have to fight but most of them are silly and just hurt us and other people. Oh God, it would be very good if you could help us to get through today without kicking anyone or spitting at anyone, or crying . . . or losing our tempers, or hurting anyone's feelings, or being very boring. (*Pause. She can't think of anything else to say.*) Amen.

SMALE and MALPASS. Amen.

(*As* ROSE *sits down,* SMALE *gives her an old-fashioned look.*)

SMALE. One more thing. Some boys in this school . . . have been doing some very bad things. They know who they are. And I know who they are. Yes. I am talking about the boys' toilets. Now some of us here are not yet five years old, and some of us are nearly seven, but I think we all know how to behave in toilets. I am not pleased about this, and you know what that means, don't you? Oh, I know who it is all right. Some silly, dirty, nasty little boys. They know who they are, and they know I know. And they will come and tell me about it, because they know they will not be forgiven unless they do. Well, we won't say any more about it now. The silly, dirty nasty little boys will come to my room, and the rest of you will be very careful about what you do in the toilets. That's all. Lead out quietly.

(ROSE *steps forward.*)

hat's it. It doesn't really take very long, but the idea is to set the tone for the day. It's a traditional assembly, as these things go. I mean, some of the sentiments are wholesome. Be good, be honest, don't pee on the wall . . . but there's got to be more than that.

SMALE. Mrs. Fidgett!

ROSE. Yes, Mrs. Smale.

SMALE. Could I have a word, Mrs. Fidgett.

ROSE. Yes, of course, Mrs. Smale. It's Ms. Strong, if you remember. Sorry.

SMALE. Oh, yes. It is rather confusing, changing your name like that, er. Ms. Strong. Don't you find it confuses the children?

ROSE. Well, I did explain it to them, Mrs. Smale and they thought it was quite a good idea. Well, it was my name first. Before I married Mr. Fidgett.

SMALE. Yes, you did explain it to me.

ROSE. And who'd be a Fidgett when they could be Strong? No, well, my husband said a Rose by any other name would smell as sweet, which was quite apt and poetic for him, but still . . . It is a point of principle with me.

SMALE. We have been through all this.

ROSE. Yes, sorry. It's just that no one seems to remember. Sorry. Not you. I know you have a lot to remember.

SMALE. Yes. While we are on points of principle, could I ask you whether it's a point of principle with you to depart from the prayers in the book, as you did this morning?

ROSE. No! Not really, Mrs. Smale, what it really was, was, I forgot it was my turn this morning and I forgot the book, so I just . . . extemporised.

SMALE. Did you.

ROSE. Didn't you like it then?

SMALE. (*Slightly thrown.*) That's not really the point, Mrs. . . . Ms. Strong. I have the parents to contend with. And the Office.

ROSE. Oh, yes, the Office.

SMALE. I think it's best if we keep to the pattern in the book, don't you? (*Turning as she goes.*) I see you've put in for one or two deputy head's posts?

ROSE. Oh, I didn't realize you'd. . .

SMALE. I've had two requests for confidential reports.

ROSE. Oh, yes. Well, yes. Thought I'd have a go.

SMALE. Thought you'd *have a go* at being a head teacher?

ROSE. That's it. You know.

SMALE. Mrs. . . . Ms. Strong. Won't you sit down.

ROSE. Thank you.

SMALE. This school is in a very difficult area, and yet it enjoys a very high reputation, no matter what you happen to think of it.

ROSE. Yes I know, Mrs. . .

SMALE. When I took it over, 10 years ago, it was a sink.

ROSE. A sink.

SMALE. I could use other words. The children were like dirty little wild animals. The staff were totally demoralized. The Director of Education took me aside: Mrs. Smale, he said, your task is to cleanse the Aegean stables. And that is what I've done. Now it's a school that parents are proud to send their children to.

ROSE. Yes, I know they are, Mrs. Smale, I never said. . .

SMALE. It can even accommodate the occasional eccentric without having its values too seriously undermined.

ROSE. I don't just undermine your values, Mrs. Smale.

SMALE. Splendid! I am very glad to hear that, Mrs. Fidgett. Well, work to do. Work to do. (*She exits.*)

ROSE. (*To audience.*) I think I handled that really well, don't you? Hm. She doesn't think I could do it. Christ you don't have to be like that to run a school, do you? Never come across a head teacher like me, though. Rose, head teacher. Seems to be a bit of a credibility gap there. Oh, come on. I just rub her up the wrong way. I mean, take the other day in the staffroom. There we were, peaceful enough scene, kettle burbling gently on the hob, fifteen glorious minutes before the start of afternoon school.

THE STAFFROOM

Three chairs. MALPASS *sits in one with* SMALE *standing behind her massaging her neck and shoulder with affectionate expertise.* ROSE *comes in and sits in another chair. She opens "The Guardian", reads it and glances towards* SMALE *and* MALPASS *every now and then. From her reactions we can gather that this massage scene is not unusual.*

MALPASS. Oh, yes, I think it's easing.
SMALE. Best not to talk, Beryl. Just try to relax.
ROSE. Headache again?

SMALE. (*Severely.*) Migraine.

ROSE. Oh. Rotten luck.

MALPASS. You're so good at it, Mrs. Smale. Much better than my husband. Really.

SMALE. It's a knack.

MALPASS. No, it's more than that. I've tried to show him so many times, and really he'd *like* to help, but he's no use at all.

SMALE. Well, I think that's often the way.

MALPASS. It's as if he's got no imagination in his fingers, as if he can't feel anything through them. Oh, yes, that's it again. There.

SMALE. Ssh.

MALPASS. And then again, I think he finds it boring.

SMALE. Well, men. They haven't got the patience. (*The kettle has boiled. She makes two cups of coffee.*) What do you say, Mrs. . . . Ms. . . . Rose?

ROSE. Some have, some haven't I suppose.

ROSE. (*Continued, to* MALPASS.) No, well, I must admit, in my limited experience, you're quite right.

MALPASS. (*Step R. to* ROSE.) Shall I tell you what started it off? My migraine?

ROSE. What?

MALPASS. That TV news last night. That case. I could feel my head starting to throb.

ROSE. What news?

MALPASS. *That case.*

ROSE. *What* case?

SMALE. *Homosexuality.*

ROSE. Oh. Oh yes.

MALPASS. To think of the children . . . *watching that*!

SMALE. Yes.

MALPASS. *On television*!

SMALE. *Yes.*

ROSE. But . . . Better than watching people kill each other. Don't you think?

SMALE. That's not the point. That's not what we were talking about.

ROSE. Well it is love, a kind of love, what if they love each other? You don't have to think about what they actually *do* if it upsets you. I mean sex is only emotions and feelings and that.

SMALE. Not for men!

ROSE. Well, I dunno. Maybe not so much. But honestly, it's ever so common.

SMALE. One in ten, I've read, but I can't credit that.

MALPASS. Oh I can. There's so much about it on television and in the papers. If people didn't hear so much about it they wouldn't have it on their minds. Some people are silly enough to try anything if they think it's the fashion.

ROSE. Oh, Beryl, you're a marvel, you make it sound like wedge heels!

(MALPASS *gets a pain.*)

You don't read in the paper and say, oh, I see, long evening skirts are out but dykes are in, I'd better rush down to the shops and get one.

(MALPASS *gets another pain.*)

SMALE. (*Crosses back to* MALPASS *and massage.*) Please! There's no need.

ROSE. I'm sorry, sorry Beryl. It's just . . . I mean if one person in ten is gay, well take the children in this school. Some of them'll grow up to be gay.

SMALE. (*Step C. to* ROSE.) You're talking about six year old boys!

ROSE. (*Crosses fil cab.*) Well I don't think it's so awful . . . I mean have lots of gay friends, I dare say you have.

SMALE. (*Back to* MALPASS *massage.*) I most certainly have not.

ROSE. Oh you have, I bet you have, but you'll never know because of the way you talk about it.

MALPASS. I'd much rather not talk about it at all.

ROSE. (*Really cross: a bit out of control.*) Well don't then cause at least you'll never hurt anyone's feelings!

MALPASS. What do you mean?

ROSE. Well, how do you know I'm not gay?

(MALPASS' *eyes jerk wide open.* SMALE *is transfixed. What* ROSE *did say was quite enough for* MALPASS.)

MALPASS. (*Hysterical.*) Because you're *married*!

(*She's really upset.* ROSE *stares at her.*)

ROSE. Sorry.

(*She picks up her copy of The Guardian.* SMALE *smoothes the shaking* MALPASS. *As the lights on them fade,* MALPASS *is beginning to relax. To the massage again. Lights up on* ROSE.)

ROSE. (*Quiet and straight: more to herself than to the audience.*) They are my sisters. They are . . . part of the sisterhood of women. And that's another scene I've buggered up. Mrs. Smale and Mrs. Malpass. I could actually get quite fond of you if only we talked the same language. I don't seem to be able to manage to talk yours. Do you think you'll ever learn mine?

SMALE. She has enthusiasm, I will say that.

MALPASS. She talks about things that are quite unnecessary.

SMALE. Her approach to the attendance register can only be described as casual.

MALPASS. I've been here two years longer than her, who does she think she is applying for deputy headships?

ROSE. I've got ideas! I want to use them!

MALPASS. She told me she thinks the reading scheme is boring and sexist!

ROSE. The only decent character's the dog!

SMALE. Relationships with colleagues, while friendly, have been marked by a certain lack of tact and reticence.

ROSE. When Smale comes to write the reference will she yield to temptation and say what she really thinks of me? Or will she write me a really good one to get me off her back?

SMALE. At present, Mrs. Fidgett has neither the dignity nor the experience for a deputy headship.

ROSE. Yeah. Right.

(MALPASS *and* SMALE *exit.*)

Still. There is one bright spark. I think my talent may have been spotted from above. From the office. Yes, "Rose Fidgett, nee Strong, and the Primary Adviser."

(BEAM *enters and stands watching. And on to next scene.*)

Now what have you got on your tables? Work cards, right. Are they ordinary work cards, Rachel? What's the matter with them then? No work on them, right. What? No *work* on the *work* cards? Help? What are we going to do? Yes, we could draw on them. Fine, anything else? We could write on them. Fine, anything else? Yes, we could make paper aeroplanes out of them. Fine. Anything else? You see, what I was thinking was, why is it always *me* doing the work cards and *you* doing the work? Yes, all right, Patrick, because I'm the teacher and you're the children. But what I thought was, you might like to have a go at being the teacher and do some work cards. D'you get it? Think of someone you'd like to do some work for you, and do them a work card. It could be anything you like, draw a rabbit, hard sums, fill in the missing work, write these letters . . . or maybe you could think of a new kind of work card. You could do one for me if you like. Yes, if you like. (*Looking at* BEAM.) Think of a question that you know the answer to and I don't. If you rack your brains you'll soon think of one. No, don't tell me. Do me a work card. OK? *Smashing.*

(JIM BEAM *threads his way through the class towards her. Scruffy—trendy—big glasses.*)

BEAM. I hope you didn't mind me sitting in on your lesson, Mrs. Strong.

ROSE. Ms.

BEAM. Sorry?

ROSE. Ms. Strong.

BEAM. (*Holding out his hand.*) Jim Beam.

ROSE. Rose Strong. Hello.

(*He takes her hand.*)

BEAM. I'm the new Primary Adviser.

(*She lets his hand go.*)

ROSE. Ah, well, I couldn't really keep you out then, could I?

BEAM. I'm sorry, I really would have preferred to ask your permission first.

ROSE. Well why didn't . . . no, it's all right. Sorry. You feel a bit of a fool. If I'd known you were coming I'd have done something different.

BEAM. Why?

ROSE. Oh, all this do your own thing. I gather it's out at the Office.

BEAM. Ah, now, it is and it isn't. The Office is a great office, and it has many mansions.

ROSE. Oh.

BEAM. I like the way you work very much.

(*There's something quite sexy about all this.*)

ROSE. Oh. (*Incredulous.*) *Do* you?

BEAM. I'll tell you something, I've had a depressing week. School after school. "This is a back to the basics school, Mr. Beam." "We're not ashamed to say we chant tables here." I've seen so much barking at print this week I could curl up.

ROSE. I make them chant tables, you know.

BEAM. Do you?

ROSE. And put their hands on their heads.

BEAM. I don't believe you.

ROSE. Oh, I do. We all do. It's the power, you see. It goes to our heads.

BEAM. I'll tell you what else you do.

ROSE. What's that then?

BEAM. You ask open questions. You're the only teacher I've seen this week who's encouraged pupil-initiated enquiry. You encourage them to predict . . . to hypothesise. I can tell you've adopted a strategy of planned intervention in their language development?

ROSE. Can you?

BEAM. At a glance. You've really absorbed the insights of the Bullock Report, haven't you?

ROSE. No, I haven't really. Not really a language person, I'm a biologist.

BEAM. I think you're a natural innovator.

ROSE. Oh. Now come on, dinosaurs! Thought you were being teachers now. Well, do teachers fight over pencils? Sorry.

BEAM. No, no. I'm taking up your time.

ROSE. It's all right. Don't talk to many grownups.

BEAM. All right if I wander round and have a look at what they're doing?

ROSE. Feel free.

BEAM. Thanks. Tell me. Why d'you call them dinosaurs and hamsters and so on?

ROSE. Oh. Stupid really. The tables choose their own names, whatever they want to be. It's just I got so fed up with red table and blue table and all that.

BEAM. (*Warmly.*) Fantastic. (*As he moves away.*)

ROSE. Watch out for the dinosaurs. They're a bit primitive.

(BEAM *moves around the tables, looking at work, as it were.* ROSE *draws a deep breath.*)

Hmm. (*She feels really pleased, when she thinks about it. Then she knots her brow. To us.*) Hang on. What *was* all that about? I had the feeling it was some sort of code. Three guesses. Not *that* again. Five more minutes, folks.

BEAM. (*To someone sitting at a table.*) No, I'm not her Father, I'm another teacher, just come to see all the good work you do. (*As he works his way back to* ROSE.) I'll come back and see you another day. (*To* ROSE.) Well, fine. Thanks for having me.

ROSE. That's OK.

BEAM. Look—I'm trying to get together a little working party of like-minded people . . . share ideas, maybe generate some new ones. I think you might be interested.

ROSE. Well. I don't know.

BEAM. I thought we might have a little initial meeting over a drink. Just an informal chat sort of thing. I'd like it if you could come along.

ROSE. Over a drink sounds promising.

BEAM. Tuesday?

ROSE. No, not Tuesday. Sorry.

BEAM. Wednesday?

ROSE. Fine. But look . . . no, never mind. Where, down the Teachers Centre?

BEAM. No, I don't think so, do you? D'you know Slops Wine Bar?

ROSE. Intimately.

BEAM. Half seven?

ROSE. Fine.

BEAM. Smashing. Well. . .

ROSE. D'you mind me asking, how many in this group so far?

BEAM. Not too many . . . Wednesday?

ROSE. Fine.

BEAM. Terrific, see you then. (*He exits.*)

ROSE. Excuse me, Ms. Strong. What was all that, no, not *Tuesday*? I mean I don't always have to go to my Mother's on Tuesdays, no I just had to say, no, not Tuesday, you don't get old Rose as easy as that Jim Beam, you've got to put yourself out for something special, but not too far cos you can have her Wednesday, I mean, why didn't I just say, Tuesday, fine! Thank you! Fancy you! Or: get lost Beam, back to the Office and play with your paper clips, but no, not Tuesday, sorry Wednesday? Oh, what a girly game. And after all that probably all he wants is a good chat about records of reading and breakthrough to literacy and here am I getting myself into some. . . Well . . . When things seem to be piling up on me a bit too fast, I hop in the car and go and see my old mate Sally. She lives about half an hour away down the bypass. And there she is, and her tatty old sofa. Been doing that ever since we were at college together; somehow we managed to get each other through all the bad bits and the boring bits, and finally, even, the finals. And then neither of us taught, not then, but right through the late sixties, when Sally was singing her songs with Jake Hardman in the U. S. of A. and I, was having kids . . . even then when ever we met, it was still O.K. (*Flopping.*) Oh, God.

SALLY. Right.

ROSE. What's happening?

SALLY. *Nothing*.

ROSE. Perfect.

SALLY. Right.

ROSE. Oh, I should live in the country.

SALLY. Yes, it's a riot of colour especially now the flashing season's started.

ROSE. Eh?

SALLY. Didn't you know? There's a season for it here. Just about when the kids start putting their marbles away, that's the flashing season. Around March the fourteenth it starts. Took me a couple of years to work it out, but it's true.

ROSE. Go on then.

SALLY. Well, wet or fine, morning, afternoon and night, the highways and byways and hedges and ditches of Warwickshire start blossoming with honest country yokels dropping their pants and flashing their compendiums. Don't laugh, I'm serious.

ROSE. No one says compendiums but you.

SALLY. I saw one today, Rose, a compendium on me way home from the library. Just been giving me chat to the Friends of the Cotswold Countryside about the natural ecology of the English hedgerow.

ROSE. Oh, I say!

SALLY. Oh yes, it had gone down a treat, and I was just strolling along, singing a merry song, as is my wont. And then this figure emerged from behind a tree, and adopted a significant pose.

ROSE. What did you do?

SALLY. Ah. Well. I'm afraid I played my part badly in this encounter. Thing is, as you know, I can hardly see a thing without my specs, and I didn't have them on. So we both sort of stood there. . . He didn't say anything and I didn't say anything. It seemed to be his move. Funny, I thought. Then I vaguely discerned there was something wrong with his pants. Has he torn them on some barbed wire, I mused innocently. Is he in need of help? Do I look like the sort of lady who carries a needle and thread about with her? So I screwed up me eyes and me courage, and peered closer. And there it was.

ROSE. His compendium!

SALLY. Shimmering vaguely through the mist. Blimey, Sally, I thought. Had again!

ROSE. Oh, Sally. How awful.

SALLY. Right. One of those really tricky problems in etiquette. I had me specs in me pockets, see. Should I put them on or not? If I did, would he be pleased at my friendly show of interest, or would he be goaded into savage animal lust—or worst of all, would he think I was trying to make some sort of satirical point about the minuscule dimensions of his compendium?

ROSE. I'd have punched him.

SALLY. You're so decisive, you. In the event, we both sort of stayed where we were, a sort of bucolic tableau, until finally he whisked back behind his tree and did a bit of grunting, and I went on me merry way.

ROSE. Why do they do it, Sally?

SALLY. A challenging question. Because they *prefer* it that way, that's why. And why do they prefer it that way I hear you asking.

ROSE. You do, you do.

SALLY. Because (*And this is the short answer.*) they are such *tremendous arseholes.*. And it's not all done behind trees either. Look, you know who came down that lane last Saturday? Only the South Warwickshire Hunt!

ROSE. Oh no.

SALLY. *Tremendous* arseholes, them. Smashed out of their skulls, skidding down the road like the charge of the Light Brigade.

ROSE. Yeah!

SALLY. Right. I actually saw the poor old fox nip down the lane, so I shut the gate and sort of leaned on it, and up comes this guy with a purple face on this gigantic charger. "Open this gate please—quickly." "No." "Open this damn gate." "Open it yourself, arsehole!"

ROSE. Right!

SALLY. Right. And then he said, "Don't you talk to me like that, get out of my bloody way!" Just like that.

But I kept my dignity. "Piss off, arsehole", I said. Go and chase something your own size!

ROSE. Great!

SALLY. (*More hesitant: re-experiencing it as it really was.*) And then . . . he just sort of stared at me. He had this look of . . . *mad hatred* in his eyes . . . and he got off his horse and walked right up to me with his whip. He really wanted to hit me with it. I thought I was going to piss myself, Rose. I had to get out of his way. . . They really hate us, you know. I think they really do hate us.

(JAKE *enters.*)

ROSE. Not all of them Sally.

SALLY. No?

ROSE. Hello, Jake.

(*He stares at her for a long time.*)

JAKE. Susan.

SALLY. Oh, Jake!

JAKE. No. (*Holds up hand to stop her telling him.*) Rose.

ROSE. That's it. How are you, Jake?

JAKE. (*Not sure.*) All right. All right.

ROSE. Seems to me you might be a little bit stoned.

SALLY. Blimey, hear that infant teacher coming out. You've got to watch that.

JAKE. What?

SALLY. She's an infant teacher.

JAKE. To teach infants . . . must be the purest delight. But what do you teach them?

ROSE. Oh, you know. Read and write.

JAKE. I wish I had never learnt to read or write. (JAKE *looks through the side table.*)

SALLY. Jake, are you looking for something?

JAKE. A bible—I was looking for a bible.

SALLY. Come here, sit down. You burnt it. Don't you remember? You took it to read on that picnic and then you lit the fire with it.

(*He stares at her, trying to remember.*)

JAKE. It doesn't matter.

(*He sits down between them and goes to sleep almost instantly.* SALLY *puts an absent minded affectionate hand on him.*)

SALLY. Sorry.

ROSE. Is he all right?

SALLY. Ah, yeah, he's got this gift of taking a catnap whenever he needs one. Mark of a great man that, Winston Churchill was just the same, Napoleon, all of them.

ROSE. Oh, Sally.

SALLY. Actually it's not the stuff so much these days, he's got this craze on Southern Comfort. Bloody expensive, but he can afford it. Wish he couldn't. Just these six songs, he could live the rest of his life on the royalties. However long that is, et cetera.

(SALLY'S *a different person with and about* JAKE: *Tender, protective, easily hurt.* ROSE *goes carefully.*)

ROSE. How . . . *is* the music?

SALLY. Oh, fine. Not bad. We're working a bit. We're doing Alcester Folk Club Saturday.

ROSE. Alcester FOLK CLUB?

SALLY. Yeah.

ROSE. (*Taking a quick look at* JAKE *to make sure he's asleep.*) But you used to do . . . well, Jake used to do. . .

SALLY. Yeah. We're unreliable now. The word is well round. It's only stage-fright, Rose, but it's spread. First it was just really big concerts he couldn't do unless he was stoned, then any stage appearance, then he had this big block about asking for things in shops.

(JAKE *wakes up suddenly, apparently sober and alert. He turns to* ROSE.)

JAKE. Hi.

ROSE. Hi.

JAKE. (*To show he remembers.*) Rose.

ROSE. That's me.

JAKE. I was thinking about a day we went to the sea. You were there. I was there. And Sally was there.

ROSE. Rhossili Beach.

JAKE. Rhossili Beach. Five miles of sand, two, no three bottles of wine, one guitar. Late September. No one on the beach except the three of us, and two little boys right down by the water.

ROSE. Oh *yes*, I remember.

JAKE. One of them had a red cap, right? And we sat there all day, drinking the wine and watching the tide come in. Till the water came right up to the blanket we were sitting on but we still didn't move, because it was so good. . .

ROSE. (*Fondly.*) I remember.

JAKE. It *was* good, all that, wasn't it? I'm going to write a song about it, Rose, now I've got it in my head, and you're going to be in it, and I'm going to be in it, and she's going to be in it, and the water's gonna be in it, and the sand . . . whassamatter?

(JAKE *looks from one to the other: The quality of their attention has changed.*)

ROSE. (*Gently.*) Jake. You wrote that song. "The Water and the Wine". You wrote that years ago.

JAKE. Oh. Yeah. Doesn't matter. What time is it?

SALLY. About half past five.

JAKE. I've got to practice. Nice seeing you Rose. Stay for a meal. We can talk.

ROSE. I don't think I can, Jake.

JAKE. You stay. You know I like to talk to you. Stay for a meal. Now I have to practice. (*He goes.*)

SALLY. Now he has to practice drinking. He hasn't got through a meal this week. Fine old performance, head in the plate by half past nine. Don't stay. It's . . . tedious for guests.

ROSE. Sally!

SALLY. I used to yearn for him at concerts all those years. Used to think, if only I could be with Jake Hardman, I could understand. If only I could get the pants off him. And then I did, and honest, it was like I thought . . . he was the most . . . the *only* really sensitive man I've ever met. He's so sensitive now he can't buy a packet of cigarettes on his own. We still make love . . . well, I make it to him. He's no tiger. But we do manage.

ROSE. Sounds all right.

SALLY. You should see us. I feel bad talking like this. I still love him. And he wrote six standards. *Six.* But I'm going to have to kick him out. I know that, Rose. (*Pause.*)

ROSE. New man came into my life today.

SALLY. (*Snapping out of it.*) Ah! Now you're talking? Did you score?

ROSE. Not there an then in the classroom. That's where it was.

SALLY. But you're going to?

ROSE. I don't know. He was very tentative.

SALLY. Well they all are these days, you don't want to stand for that. What was he like? Did he have a big dick?

ROSE. Amazing.

SALLY. You stand no nonsense from him then. Get his pants off.

ROSE. He has got a very nice face, too.

SALLY. Now don't you start turning into a face woman, Rosie Ridgett, you can't afford to weaken. Start getting soft with them, they take advantage, use their little wheedling ways with you, and before you know where you are, you're caught. Like me.

ROSE. And me. I have got this husband, you know.

SALLY. Oh, yes. Keep forgetting him.

ROSE. So do I. The little man.

SALLY. The old ball and chain.

ROSE. Nice to have someone to come home to though.

SALLY. So long as you keep 'em right there.

ROSE. And they love you for it.

SALLY. Toss 'em the odd word.

SALLY and ROSE. *Shut up*!

ROSE. Bit of a cuddle now and then.

SALLY. But you can't let 'em trap you.

ROSE. You got to be hard with them.

SALLY. Cruel to be kind.

ROSE. Only language they understand.

SALLY. As for this guy, you've got to put it straight. Look, you've got a sweet face, but I'm a married woman.

ROSE. I've got a family and responsibilities.

SALLY. We could be great together, but no emotional involvement.

ROSE. Not the starry eyed type.

SALLY. I'll be frank, you know my motto about men?

SALLY and ROSE. Find 'em, feel 'em, fuck 'em, and forget 'em! (*Pause. They subside.*)

SALLY. Seriously, though, do it, Rose.

ROSE. D'you reckon? D'you think that's the answer?

SALLY. Oo, ar. Wouldn't go as far as that. But look at it this way: what else is there to do? While you've still got most of you teeth like.

ROSE. Ar.

SALLY. Ar.

ROSE. Ar. (ROSE *comes away.*) Sally does exhilarate me. "I'm going to have to kick him out". What an exhilirating phrase. I like the drive home too: country lanes first, then bombing along the bypass, carving it up with all those little salesmen in their cars. I think it's a smashing road, that bypass, I won't have a word said against it. And I'm thinking I'm going to have to kick him out, hell, Sally can do it, I can do it, and my foot's hard down on the floor and the road ahead is clear, Vroom! And then I'm slowing up for the roundabout, and it's all changing down and thirty mile limit, and what a careful lady I've become. There's a sign just before you get to our road that's always *puzzled* me; it says, Dead slow, altered priorities ahead. And dead slow my little car obediently goes, nosing down our avenue, past the weeping cherries, into the carport, snug as a hamster, and I switch off and the engine dies. I don't know what you're like with your husband. This is what we're like.

ROSE. (*Coming in.*) Sorry, sorry I'm late.

GEOFFREY. Fine. No problem.

ROSE. I went to see Sally. I left a note for the kids.

GEOFFREY. I read it.

ROSE. I tried to phone you. . .

GEOFFREY. Did you?

ROSE. No. I nearly did but then I just went. Sorry. Are you cross?

GEOFFREY. No.

ROSE. I mean, if you are, do say. I would.

GEOFFREY. Nothing to be cross about. Everything's fine. I coped.

ROSE. Kids all right?

GEOFFREY. Fine.

ROSE. You're a good lad.

GEOFFREY. Thank you.

ROSE. Where are they.

GEOFFREY. Sarah's watching telly.

ROSE. Done her flute practice?

GEOFFREY. (*Wearily.*) Yes.

ROSE. What about Alex?

GEOFFREY. Homework. He's only just gone up. He

had whatsisname, Huggie, round earlier. Swapping things, or selling things. Don't worry. Everything's fine.

ROSE. Sure?

(*She means sure you feel all right about it? He takes it as meaning sure you could manage.*)

GEOFFREY. There's not a lot to tax the brain about getting supper and washing it up, Rose. About two minutes thought and ten minutes effort I'd say. (*A tinge of irritated contempt implied.*)

ROSE. Well that's super.

GEOFFREY. I mean if I couldn't apply critical path analysis I'd soon be up shit creek at work, wouldn't I? There's a problem, and a time to solve it in. The problem's hunger, right?

(*We sense how boring and narrow he can be at work.*) The special circumstances are that the time factor's crucial. Because there's been a breakdown at stage one. Buying the raw material. Right?

ROSE. We had eggs.

GEOFFREY. We didn't feel like eating eggs.

ROSE. Intrusion of consumer resistance?

GEOFFREY. If you like, Rose. So we needed to come up with something that had a very short A to B factor, but would still satisfy the basic specification.

ROSE. So what did you come up with?

GEOFFREY. Sent Alex out for fish and chips.

ROSE. Ah! Brilliant.

GEOFFREY. I mean it bloody amuses me the mystique some women make out of what's basically such a mundane area. All that house stuff, it's so trivial Rose, all it wants is a bit of applied analysis and you can see it off in no time, give yourself room for something a bit more important.

ROSE. Yes, I see, thank you Geoffrey.

GEOFFREY. No trouble.

ROSE. What's more important tonight then?

GEOFFREY. Well I do happen to have a hell of a lot of paperwork to shift tonight.

ROSE. Oh. Sorry.

GEOFFREY. Just sorting one of Targett's little schemes for him.

ROSE. Oh. I was hoping we might have a bit of a chat.

GEOFFREY. Yes, well, fine. I'll see what I can do. About how long were you thinking?

(*She looks at him.*)

ROSE. Hadn't actually worked it out in minutes.

GEOFFREY. I have got quite a bit of work to do.

ROSE. Tough day at work, was it.

GEOFFREY. Nothing that can't be sorted.

(*Pause. Maybe she starts to speak but he is into his stride.*)

See, I get to the office this morning, first cup of coffee, settle down to knock off a few notes for the board meeting on Monday; that new feller strolls in — Target: y'know, the golden boy from Head Office—and he's got a *title* now: "Director of Personnel"—which leaves the Personnel *Manager* in a funny position . . . Anyway, he chucks a file *that* thick on my desk. Just skim through that, old boy—welcome any insights that float to the surface . . . Skim through! There's only about ten hours extra work there . . . Thank you very much Mr. Target, sir . . . Prick! (*With a two fingered gesture.*) So, I'm just sharpening my pencils when little Anderson trots in—you know him, he's got that girl friend with a funny eye—"Ooh sorry Geoffrey, got to take that file away, need a few copies run off!" "Fine. Have it with my blessings", I said. Just let me have it back by 5 o'clock so I can take it home and have *a really good weekend*. . ."

ROSE. Oh dear. . .

GEOFFREY. Right. . . (*He gets up to help himself to a drink: a man from the world of commerce, under pressure.*)

ROSE. Look Geoff, on the way back from Sally's. . .

GEOFFREY. No hang on, I haven't got to it yet. . . Halfway through the afternoon, Target's back. "Got anything on that file yet, Geoffrey?" "Well not a lot," I said. "You had it back off me half-an-hour after you put it down. . ." "*Surely* not?" "Anderson's had the bloody thing in the copy room all day!", I said. "Oh well, never mind, give it a miss now, eh Geoff? Be exciting to have your first impressions at the meeting on Monday . . . have a nice weekend!" . . . Oh yes! . . . So he's got the file, and we're both due in a board meeting Monday morning to discuss it: all I've read is "Page One: Introduction!" Well, *Mr.* Target's in for a little surprise . . . a *new* report from Geoffrey Fidgett, that *he* hasn't read—see how he likes that! I'm going to crack it tonight, from first principles. . .

ROSE. So you've got a lot of work on.

GEOFFREY. I've just been . . . no, never mind. I can cope.

ROSE. I was listening, honest. (*Pause.*) Actually, if you're working I can have a crack at that reading scheme.

GEOFFREY. Oh yes? Good dog Nip, eh?

ROSE. Come, Nip, come! See! Nip comes. He's about the only one who bloody does. It's a terrible world in these reading schemes, Geoff.

GEOFFREY. (*He's heard it before.*) Oh, yeah.

ROSE. See Peter help Daddy wash the car. See Jane help mummy dust.

GEOFFREY. Bit dull, yeah.

ROSE. Bit dull, it's bloody criminal. Wait till I get mine out! Jane likes to fight. Peter has a new doll. Mum is out. Mum likes fun. She is fond of a treat. Dad will get the chips. Dad can crack it. Dad can cope fine.

(*Little pause.*)

GEOFFREY. Are you in for the night then now?

ROSE. Yes, I think so.

GEOFFREY. I was thinking I might go out for a drink when I've done that lot.

ROSE. Do. You owe it to yourself. Unless you fancy staying home.

GEOFFREY. *What*?

ROSE. I thought we might have an evening in. Drink a bottle of wine. Couple of bottles.

GEOFFREY. It's a bad night on the telly.

ROSE. I meant. . . (*She's embarrassed.*) I mean . . . perhaps we could spend an evening together. You know. *Talk* and that.

GEOFFREY. Oh. (*Trying to muster a response to this surprising suggestion.*) Yes! Fine! If you like. . .

ROSE. It's all right, you don't have to.

GEOFFREY. (*Seizing.*) Your mother was round earlier. She thought you'd be in. Of course I wasn't able to tell her where you were.

ROSE. What did she want?

GEOFFREY. I don't know.

ROSE. What did she say?

GEOFFREY. She said I hope she remembers she's married.

ROSE. Oh. S'pose I'd better go round and see her. If I go now, you could go out for a drink a bit later.

GEOFFREY. Right. Unless you really want an evening in.

ROSE. No. It's all right. It really doesn't matter.

GEOFFREY. Fine.

(*She stands there looking at him. He looks up. She looks back at him. He turns away. Light off* GEOFFREY.)

ROSE. Um . . . coming back from my mothers, I had this . . . odd visual experience. The light was on in the kitchen, and I could see my husband, working away, with his briefcase open on the table. He looked up . . . he must have heard me . . . stared blindly in my direction; and suddenly I felt that what he was going to do was to climb right inside his case and shut the lid over himself. So that he wouldn't have to talk to me. (ROSE *pauses, continues.*) And all that weekend, all through the girls playing flutes and the boys playing football and the carving and eating of the Sunday roast, that's where he stayed. In his case. The thing about school is that you have to go there every day. It's the only way they have of doing it. And that's quite nice, knowing where you have to be, that that's where they are, the kids, and the teachers all in it together. It to them, and they eat and ate it, though they didn't we to, so as not to hurt my feelings, and we were all so *nice* and *calm* and *patient* I could feel some sort of big soft explosion welling up inside my head and I dragged poor old Sarah off for a long trudge in a muddy wood that she could well have done without. As we came back, I looked through the window, and saw my husband, becalmed at his desk. And I had this sudden disturbing memory of something I'd seen in a film about Darwin—a giant turtle fossil welded to a rock in the Galapagos Islands. (*Pause. Now she's really talking to the Audience.*) The thing about school is that you have to go there every day. It's the only way they have of doing it. And that's quite nice, knowing where you have to be, that that's where they are, the kids, and the teachers all in it together.

THE STAFFROOM

MALPASS *is in there putting on lipstick. When* ROSE *comes in there she puts it away as if she's ashamed of it or something.*

ROSE. Oh, God, Monday.
MALPASS. I'm sorry?
ROSE. Nothing. Just, Monday. You know.

MALPASS. Oh. (*Making an effort.*) Yes, I know.

ROSE. Though, that's an awful thing to say, I mean, there they are, they really look forward to seeing us, some of them, we should. . .

MALPASS. Yes.

ROSE. How's the headache now? I mean, the migraine.

MALPASS. (*Tight.*) Much better, thank you.

ROSE. Really?

MALPASS. Yes, really; much better.

ROSE. I'm . . . sorry if I upset you, Friday. I've been thinking about it.

MALPASS. You didn't upset me. (*She did.*)

ROSE. No, it was rotten. I didn't mean to. I mean, it's enough of a strain, being with the kids all day. . . I don't know what your husband does, but mine goes and sits in an office, and a girl brings him coffee, and if he wants to, he can go out for half an hour, and nobody comes and plagues him for spellings, nobody's sick on the floor, not even at the office party. . .

MALPASS. Rolls-Royce.

ROSE. What?

MALPASS. My husband works there.

ROSE. Oh, yes. In the office?

MALPASS. Drawing Office.

ROSE. Yes, well, there you are. They don't know.

MALPASS. They don't know *anything*.

(*She's come out too much and feels the need to withdraw: She finds some physical way of doing it.*)

ROSE. So, really, I mean, I'm sorry. It's a hard life, we ought to stick together.

MALPASS. You don't seem to find it hard. You just . . . sail through it.

ROSE. I don't. Honest. I'm just whistling in the dark. I think I know what's right to do but people keep telling me I'm wrong, and bloody parents come up and say I'm very worried about Sharon, and I think that's *her child*, and what have I done about Sharon except hear her read and stop Garth hitting her, and so on, multiplied by *thirty-five*.

MALPASS. I didn't know you felt like that.

ROSE. Well I do. But then I think we all do but we feel we've got to hide it . . . it's as if there's something stopping you from being yourself when you're in school, and that's not right . . . is it? I mean, it should be possible to let things show . . . even weaknesses, I think the kids could take it.

MALPASS. I don't think I could do that. (*She's fiddling nervously.*) Not sure that I could.

ROSE. Hey, look, did you meet the primary advisor bloke on Friday?

MALPASS. He did come in.

ROSE. He was nice, wasn't he? Well, he seemed all right to me. He stayed and talked for quite a bit, he seemed really sympathetic. He's trying to get some sort of discussion group going, starting Wednesday. Why don't you come?

MALPASS. Oh no, I don't think I could. It's Derek's snooker night and I usually do my hair and have an early night.

ROSE. Well let him do his hair for once on a Wednesday. Come on, why not? I'm going.

MALPASS. I'm not applying for deputy headships.

ROSE. It's not that. It's a chance to talk, get ideas, get things, you know, off your chest. . .

MALPASS. No! It's not really my sort of thing.

ROSE. Well you could make it your sort of thing. And he's not like the rest of that lot, he's a human being, he's nice.

MALPASS. (*Very tight.*) If it's of any interest to you, he stood at the back of my classroom for ten minutes and walked out without saying a word! (*She goes Off.*)

ROSE. In my line of business you often come across stories about little girl animals, who set off to see the world, have adventures, take control, put themselves about a bit, you know. And they always, always find that the world is full of scary foxes and big, bad wolves, and they are jolly glad to scamper back to the cosy farm. It's not like that, it is not like that! All the foxes are frightened and all the wolves round here are on valium. I walk down the garden path. I open the gate and I say "Hello world, Rose here" and all you can see for miles are furry bottoms disappearing down burrows. I do not mean any harm, I just want things to be real. Where is everybody? I just want to be myself, that's all. Will someone tell me what's so frightening about that? (*Pause. Quietly.*) I just felt like talking to someone, that's all.

MOTHER. (*This like the other voices comes from outside the circle as it were.*) I know it's not for me.

MALPASS. (*Quiet and deadly.*) You can't help me.

BEAM. You've really absorbed the insights of the Bullock Report.

JAKE. I wish I'd never learnt to read and write.

SMALE. Work to do, work to do.

GEOFFREY. Critical path—not to worry, it's all cracked—forget it.

SALLY. I'm really going to have to kick him out.

MALPASS. I'm not like you.

ROSE. Look, this is not fair.

GEOFFREY. (*Wearily.*) No problem. I sent Alex down the chip shop.

ROSE. And what do *you* want?

GEOFFREY. It's all right. It really doesn't matter.

ROSE. (*Long pause.*) Fine. (*She looks up.*)

END OF ACT ONE

ACT II

Rose *sitting at her bedroom table in a slip. Getting made up.*

Her Mother *sits in her hat and coat, watching her.*

Mother. I'll tell you what, Rose, you want to get that bit of wood fixed downstairs by your front door.

Rose. Do I?

Mother. Yes, you want to get that fixed soon. It's all loose, I keep thinking I'm going to fall over it, and it makes the door stick. And it's going to bring the edge of the carpet up soon if it's not done. I notice it's fraying now.

Rose. (*Moans.*) Oohhhhh.

Mother. Well it won't do itself will it?

Rose. I was hoping it might sort of settle down of its own accord.

Mother. It's going to ruin that carpet *and* force the hinges loose on your front door, *and* someone's going to trip over it and have a nasty fall. Mrs. Garbey's next door was like that, and I told her you want to get that seen to, and she said I'm meaning to, and then she fell over it herself and broke her shoulder. I went to see her in hospital and she said you were quite right, I should have listened to you. I took her one of those cakes from Elizabeth the Chef but I don't think she ate it. I hate waste. All you need is a couple of screws!

Rose. Oh, mother is that really all I need?

MOTHER. No need to be sarky with me, you don't suit it, never did.

ROSE. Sorry

MOTHER. I date it from the time you stopped calling me mummy and started this mother business.

ROSE. You called your mother 'mother'.

MOTHER. Well we did then. Has Geoffrey got a countersink punch?

ROSE. Has Geoffrey got a what?

MOTHER. A countersink punch.

ROSE. Gosh I don't know. I rather doubt it.

MOTHER. Because unless he countersinks those screws they'll stick up and catch the door and he'll have achieved *nothing*! Your father always used to countersink his screws. You want to tell Geoffrey to be sure and countersink his screws, or they'll catch the door.

ROSE. I knew there was something I wanted to tell him but I didn't realise it was that!

MOTHER. You know I don't mean to interfere, Rose.

ROSE. Sorry.

MOTHER. I was just trying to give you a hint.

ROSE. Yes, I know, I ought to have a go at it. Stuff like that, I just wish it would go away, and little jobs seem to depress old Geoff out of all proportion.

MOTHER. He does want to get that job done though.

ROSE. No, mother, he doesn't. If the door jammed shut for ever he'd just walk round the back? Why don't *you* ask him?

MOTHER. (*Shocked.*) Oh, I couldn't do that. (*Pause, then as if discussing an embarrassing disability.*) He's not very mechanically minded, is he?

ROSE. No.

MOTHER. No. Still, I suppose some men aren't. (*Pause.*) We were forty years in that house in Melton Avenue and we never had to have a man in.

ROSE. I know.

MOTHER. Ours was the only house that had its guttering cleaned out twice a year. The only one.

ROSE. Mm.

MOTHER. And then it didn't seem to add anything to the value when we came to sell it. Will he be wanting to come in?

ROSE. Who?

MOTHER. Your husband.

ROSE. Well if he does, he will.

MOTHER. I mean will he want to get changed.

ROSE. Well if he does, he will.

MOTHER. I don't want to be in the way.

ROSE. You're not in the way.

MOTHER. I can't seem to get relaxed tonight. Is this what you're wearing?

ROSE. Mm. Thought so.

MOTHER. Is it a dance then?

ROSE. I told you, it's a *meeting*.

MOTHER. Not much of that for a meeting, is there. You'll catch your death, that's thinner than what we'd wear to dances in the Oxford Rooms. Why don't you wear, that other thing, that jersey dress, I'd have thought you'd have suited that better for a meeting. Still I don't know what these meetings are like.

ROSE. Not sure I do.

MOTHER. Will there be many there?

ROSE. Not a lot, I gather.

MOTHER. Don't you think you go to too many of these meetings, you hardly ever seem to stop home these days. I don't know what you'd do without me to babysit. Baby sit. Alex is bigger than me!

ROSE. They love having you here. Honest.

MOTHER. Yes, well if that's all I'm any use for I might as well do it; still I'm surprised you want to turn out on a night like this, after working all day, you must be fond of a treat.

ROSE. I am.

MOTHER. Yes, well, so long as you remember you're married.

(ROSE *pulls a face.*)

You know, I was wearing one a bit like this when I met your father. That was in the Oxford rooms. He was a lovely dancer. Very light on his feet. Well, he always wore his pumps. Not all of them did, but he did. I was longing for him to ask me to dance, and then he did, it was the Moonlight Saunter, I can remember it now, we hadn't got twice round the room before I felt something give.

ROSE. What?

(*As* MUM *gets into her story you can see what a bright young girl she was.*)

MOTHER. The elastic on my drawers. It happened that quick they were down round my ankles before you could say knife. Step out of them, he said. Quick as that. I can hear him now. Step out of them. And I did, and he had them in his pocket that quick on one knew what was going on. Well I couldn't look him in the face after that, I managed to keep going round just till that dance was finished, like, just so nobody would notice anything, and then I ran away to hide from him, spent the whole evening in the ladies cloakroom. Nobody knew what was the matter with me.

ROSE. Oh, mother.

MOTHER. But at the end he was waiting for me on the steps. I've got something of yours, you know he said. You didn't think I'd let you go without me, did you? And he just took my arm. He never told anybody about it, you know Rose. He was a real gentleman.

ROSE. Was it . . . um. . . (*It's difficult, but she feels she's rarely been this close.*) Was it very good with him?

MOTHER. Well, Rose, you know I thought the world of him. Oh I see, you mean what they call the physical side.

Well, I don't think we bothered so much about all that then. He was a very shy man, you know Rose, very modest. I was myself.

ROSE. I used to think, you know, he was sort of against all that.

MOTHER. Oh, no. Mind you, like I say, he was a very modest man. I sometimes used to wish he was more . . . but there, you can't wish for the moon. He never badly used me, you know, and he was never . . . I think in a way he set too much store by it, if you know what I mean Rose.

ROSE. Yes.

MOTHER. He was very fond of you, your dad. Nothing was too good for our little Rose.

ROSE. I know.

MOTHER. I keep thinking Geoffrey'll be wanting to come in.

ROSE. Well if he does he will.

MOTHER. I mean he'll want to get changed. He might want to change his trousers, Rose.

ROSE. We might get lucky.

MOTHER. Well it wouldn't do for me to see him in his birthday suit, now would it?

ROSE. I don't suppose he'd mind, mother.

MOTHER. No, they don't now, do they? You know, your father would never let me see him naked. He was very modest about that, he'd always lock the bathroom door, except, you know, the last couple of years. It seems a shame in a way Rose, he had a lovely build.

ROSE. Yes, I know.

MOTHER. Not till right near the end, you know, when I had to wash him and change him and everything. I think that was the first time I'd ever got a proper look at him, and even then, you know, when I had to wash his, you know, his peenuss, even when he was helpless, he'd try t brush my hand off, he thought it was all wrong. . . (*She* is unconsciously doing the brushing off movement.) and I almost had to laugh, of course it hadn't been any danger for years. . . We'd been brought up to think it was ugly, Rose, but it wasn't ugly, really, not even then. They're quite bonny really when you get your eye in for them, don't you think Rose. Seemed such a waste. Are you laughing at me?

ROSE. No, I'm not. You never said anything like that to me before.

MOTHER. Yes, well, doesn't matter what I say now, does it like?

ROSE. Wish you had before.

MOTHER. Yes, well we didn't then did we? Mind, I think it's best now what you young ones do, talk it out in the open. And I'm fond of a good chat. Well it puts the time in. I'm stopping you getting on, and your husband'll want to get changed. I'll go down to see to the bairns now, Rose.

ROSE. Mum, d'you ever think . . . well, that it's all been set up so that no one gets what they want?

MOTHER. Well of course it is, the secret's not expecting too much from it, eh, is that the time, I've missed Dallas. (*She goes.*)

(ROSE *sighs.*)

ROSE. Oh, mother. Talking was never your problem. You always seemed to be able to decide what you'd say and when. It's me. I can talk a bit to the kids, I can talk a bit to Sally, but I can't say things to Geoffrey, it's too hard when you've been married so long. And I could never in a million years say "Oh, mother can't you see, you may have a dead husband, but I've got a dead marriage!" (*That with great force and conviction. Pause.*) Silly cow. Dead marriage. Sounds like a dead hamster. Darling. Yes, darling? Can you smell something funny under the sideboard, darling? Oh, don't worry darling, it's only a dead marriage. Anyway, our marriage is not dead. It's only half dead.

(GEOFFREY *comes in. He's been having a bath and is wearing a short, old, cheap-looking shiny dressing gown over nothing. He comes and stands behind her, stooping to comb his hair in the imaginary mirror.*)

Oh I say, you do look spruce.

GEOFFREY. Ha.

ROSE. You must be the cleanest man in the Midlands tonight. You were in there so long I thought you were going to soak your toenails off.

GEOFFREY. Ha, ha ha ha ha. (*Hollow. He goes and sits down where* MOTHER *sat. It's either a bed or something that would do for a bed: maybe* SALLY's *couch converts. He sits down and sort of goes into a vacant trance.*)

(ROSE *cranes to see him in the mirror.*)

ROSE. Right little barrel of fun tonight. Come on, it can't be that bad. What's on for tonight, then?

GEOFFREY. (*Very quickly.*) Meeting.

ROSE. Oh.

GEOFFREY. What have you got on tonight?

ROSE. Meeting.

GEOFFREY. Ah.

ROSE. That's that, then. (*To Audience.*) I will say this for him, he does look after his clothes. He's had that ratty old dressing gown ever since I've known him. He proposed to me in that dressing gown. That was in what I think of as my mucky period. I was a keen young biology student, and I used to go and visit him in this flat. Ooh, what a mucky flat it was. We'd just lie about, him and me, me and my dirty lover in his dirty room, and I loved it, I was really being the dirty little bugger my dad said I was, and it was nice, I really really loved him and his flat, I think he hoped I'd clean it up for him, but I wasn't having that, I liked it just as it was, him and me, lying about in the dust and gloom being dirty . . . and then one day he proposed to me.

(They are lying behind the bed. Satisfied noises "Oh, yes!" Then GEOFFREY *feels on bed for cigs. Sits up, lights cig, lies down, giving it to* ROSE, *sits up again, looks down, looks worried, searches around on bed.)*

GEOFFREY. Oh, Christ.

ROSE. What?

GEOFFREY. Well, I seem to have lost it.

ROSE. What?

GEOFFREY. *(After having a brief look.)* Seems to have come off inside you.

ROSE. *(Puzzled.)* Eh? *(Realizing.)* What? *(Leaping off the bed.)* What are we going to do? I've got to wash it out!

GEOFFREY. I don't think you can do that!

ROSE. Well I've got to do something!

GEOFFREY. Probably be all right.

ROSE. Oh, Geoffrey! I'm going down the bathroom!

GEOFFREY. OK.

ROSE. Well, come with me then.

GEOFFREY. You know where it is.

ROSE. Oh you mean bugger, you know I'm frightened to light that gas heater.

GEOFFREY. It's simple.

ROSE. Well come with me then. We've got to be quick.

(He doesn't move.)

Oh, you mean bugger.

(She rushes off. GEOFFREY *lights a cigarette. Pause.)*

Geoffrey, I can't find the matches.

GEOFFREY. On the window sill.

(Pause. Then a big dull bang. [If you can do it without the bang so much the better.] GEOFFREY *jumps off the bed.* ROSE *totters back on.)*

ROSE. It exploded. You mean bugger. You wouldn't come with me. (*She is shaking.*)

GEOFFREY. It's all right. We'll get married.

(*They stand still for a moment facing each other, then* GEOFFREY *sits down on the bed again slowly.* ROSE *goes back to the mirror.*)

ROSE. Yes. And I could have said no, but as my mother said, with a bairn on the way your choices are a bit cut down like, and my father wouldn't speak to me at all for months and well, I did love him and his dust and his dressing gown. Come on it can't be that bad. Get your trousers on.

(*Holds them out.* GEOFFREY *gets up grabs them, and goes out.* ROSE *picks up the dress and pulls it on.*)

Trouble with you, Rose, you want it all on a plate, don't you. Yes. That would be a very convenient way of having it. Always ready with a slick answer. Don't you realise you've got to work at your marriage? We have done, we have done. We've always done our own servicing. Workshop Manual, good set of tools, you can fix anything. Coming down the pub for a jar, Geoffrey? No, no, Saturday mornings we always do a bit of work on the old marriage, you know. It's a kind of hobby with us. Oh, yes. Any time you liked, you could come round and found us working on our marriage. You know. Lying underneath it with our feet sticking out. Only in recent years have we had to seek any outside help. Oh, Rose. Who's going to fancy you in that? Jim Beam the Primary School Adviser, that's who. Think positive. (*She squirts perfume, on her neck, behind her ears, down the front of her dress and on an afterthought at the top of her thighs . . . and goes out of the room, switching off the light as she goes.*)

(*Wine bar music.*)

(*Light comes up very slowly on* JIM BEAM *threading his way through the tables to the one where* ROSE *is sitting. He is carrying a bottle.*)

ROSE. Another *bottle*?

BEAM. Well, you know the sort of stuff they sell by the glass.

ROSE. Oh, yes. Casa Rotaguta. Well, this is very nice. I ought to pay for this one though.

BEAM. Oh, no no no.

ROSE. Are we on expenses?

BEAM. I have a Puritan conscience about expenses.

ROSE. And everything else, I trust. Funny how the rest of the like-minded people didn't show up.

BEAM. It seems like-minded people are few and far between in this town.

ROSE. *People* are few and far between in this town. Grown up people, anyway. (*She looks around.*) D'you know I think we might be the only ones in this place of legal drinking age? Go on, pour away. I've got hollow legs.

BEAM. The girl at the bar said a strange thing to me—I asked her if she had any nuts! Do you know what she said? "Do I look as if I've got any nuts!" No, it's very disturbing for the linquistic philosopher.

ROSE. Sounds to me as if you might be in there, I'll keep your seat if you like.

BEAM. No thanks! I'm fine where I am. (*Pause as he pours.*) Actually, I think my Puritan conscience can square with the *first* bottle on expenses. This one's personal.

ROSE. Does that mean we can stop talking about language development in the integrated day now?

BEAM. If we like, yes.

ROSE. What's all this about, then?

(*He takes a drink.*)

BEAM. You're very direct, aren't you?

ROSE. Weren't they like that in Bristol?

BEAM. Oh, no. Very devious, Bristolians.

ROSE. Sorry. I didn't used to be like this. I am now though. With new people. It's my policy. It's only with new people, I can't be like this with the old ones. You get trapped in these games and routines and you can't get out of them.

BEAM. How's it working out so far?

ROSE. What?

BEAM. Being direct, with the new people.

ROSE. I dunno yet, you're the first. What's it all about then?

BEAM. Well . . . it's about pleasure, I suppose. Um . . . getting to know each other. Feeling our way? (*He's drinking more.*)

ROSE. I've accelerated your alcohol consumption. And you haven't even said anything yet.

BEAM. But it is like that. Isn't that how it has to be?

ROSE. I dunno, I hoped there might be some other way.

BEAM. (*Taking her hand.*) You're very nice, you know. I'm very glad I met you.

(*She looks at their hands, looks at him, begins to speak, hesitates, strokes his hand with the other hand, changes her mind, speaks after all.*)

ROSE. Yes, I s'pose you're quite right, really. I mean you can't just fall on me like King Rat even supposing you wanted to. I mean we have to send out these little messages in code and see if we like the feel of each other's hands and see if we laugh at the same jokes, even though it's very hard to listen to what's coming out of our mouths. Because the main thing on our minds is does she do it and will she for me, and will she tonight, sorry if I'm being embarrassing and barking up the wrong tree if that's the right phrase, because I'm just extrapolating from my own feeling, just ordinary woman feelings like do I look all right and does he actually fancy me or is he just pretending or is he just being polite, and if not is he going to make a move and if so when's he going to make it. See?

BEAM. (*Smiling.*) Go on.

ROSE. Well you see all that implies that we've got to sit here in this alcoholic youth club and finish up all that wine and maybe even a brandy or two until they turn on those horrible interrogation-type spotlights they have in all these places, and we're caught in the glare like a police raid or something, and then we know it's really time to go, and you really have to say something, or not, or maybe I have to say something, but let's assume it's you, because you seem to be the sort of guy who takes charge, you are the Primary Adviser after all.

BEAM. So what do I say?

ROSE. Well, let's see, you are the Primary Adviser and a devious Bristolian so you can't say, Rose, I'd really like to screw you or anything like that, no, it'll still be in code, like have you got time for a coffee back at my place, right? And I won't say what for, I've got plenty of coffee at home and anyway I prefer a cup of tea after I've been drinking, no, I wouldn't do any of that, I'd say mm, yes, that would be very nice, and give you one of those code smiles, and you'd think pow! Beam scores again! Or does he? Because there's still lots and lots to go through, like when we get outside and there's two cars and not one, now do I follow you in my car or do we both go in yours? Tricky, that, because if we take the two cars you won't have to turn out afterwards and take me back to the car park, and that could be a very sticky journey as well as inconvenient if the stuff at your place didn't turn out according to plan, but then again, if we both go in the one car at least we know I'm going to get to the place, and we can hold hands on the way and create some sort of atmosphere of pleasurable expectancy, although we're both furiously thinking our own thoughts all the way, and you keep having to let go of my hand to change gear.

BEAM. My car is automatic!

ROSE. Ah, well, I can see you've made your mind up about the transport arrangements then. So there we are back at your place, and the door closes behind us, and then what? Do you take me in your arms straight away, or do you bustle off and actually make this coffee you've been talking about? Well, maybe both, first one, then the other, cos you've got class, you're not a bull at a gate man, I can see that, so off you go to make the coffee and I wander round have a look at your books and that, until I get lonely and nervous after about thirty seconds and follow you into the kitchen, and surprise, it turns out to be brandy as well as coffee, or maybe Scotch, something anyway, and we go back in the living room and sit and sip and do a lot of eye contact, and then . . . And then . . . Yes, music. I wonder if you happen to get off on Bob Marley you say in a casual sort of way, and that would be a shrewd move on your part because I do, hint, hint, and then some more eye contact, and then maybe even a bit of slow dancing it's a bit old fashioned but it's good for the old body contact and it gives us a few clues on how we might . . . you know.

BEAM. Go on.

ROSE. And then it's really time, no going back, eh? And I'm wondering are you the sort of chap who likes to take all my clothes off one by one very slowly or is it one each side of the bed undressing race, on your marks get set off. It's all right, you don't have to say now. Anyway, there we are, finding out who's got the coldest feet, doing our absolute level best to oblige, and then it's over, well I'm not implying as quick as all that but that is one of those things you absolutely can't predict, and anyway, we both say it was really super, even if it wasn't . . . but maybe . . . maybe it really was. (*Pause.*) But, even if it really was, we still have to get up, and you have to drive me back to my car, because I do have a husband and kids at home, and I can't stay with you, Jim. (*Pause.*)

BEAM. Is that it, then?

ROSE. No, no, it's not, that the trouble, because you can't leave it at that, can you, not civilised people like us, got to see each other again, even if it's just out of politeness, and then me being what I am, I'd stop being nervous about it and really get to like it, and we'd find out what we really like to do together, and, oh, there'd be all that smashing awful bit where I can't wait to see you, and hanging round the center hoping you might be doing a bit of shopping, and turning round every time a car like yours goes by, God I hope you don't drive a bus, and all that trying not to be the first one to say I love you, and trying not to look at my watch and trying not to notice when you do, and all that bloody compulsive *buying* you things . . . And anyway, it's double complicated with you because of all the old Primary Adviser bit and my relentless surging ambition to rise high in the Infant School Mafia, and I can get you into interviews, baby, I could make you one of the really headmistresses, the old Puritan conscience is going to take a terrible hammering, mine too. All that having to feel in the mood whenever we're together because we can't be together often and it's a shame to waste the time, so sooner or later one of us starts having to fake it. . .

BEAM. Men can't fake it.

ROSE. What?

BEAM. Men. They can't fake it.

ROSE. Yes. Right! So then we're into all that, what's the matter, nothing's the matter, funny never happened to me before, it's so pretty when it's small, oh God is that the time, you know, all that, and then again, and the writing's on the wall, and someone has to call it a day, or do we really get down and work on it, but that's just like working on your marriage, and I've done that, rather work on the track at Chrysler. So . . . best to let it go. Say we'll always be friends and then avoid each other. I mean when you look at it, like that it hardly seems worth starting. The thing is I *do* want more and I *do* want my life to change, but I don't see you and me bringing the revolution any closer. Even though it seems like the only option at the moment so maybe I ought to take it. (ROSE *takes a sip.*) I wish you'd say something, Jim, I'm getting this awful feeling of foreboding creeping over me that maybe you didn't have anything like that in mind at all, maybe I'm going crackers and I can't read the signals any more, but I got so nervous I just had to say it. I'm really sorry. Spoiling your evening and that. Please say something. You've got to tell me. Was I completely up the creek?

(*The lights come up very bright. Pause.*)

BEAM. Only in detail. You see, I'm married too. Can't take you back. Thought we might do it in the car. (*Pause.*)

ROSE. (*Laughs.*) OK. (ROSE'S *bedroom. She comes in. Dark. Softly.*) Geoffrey? You asleep? Geoff? (*She puts the light on. He's not there.*) Blimey. Long meeting. Longer than mine. Could he have forgotten he's married, I ask myself. (*She takes her dress off and flops down on to the chair. Looks in mirror.*) You look . . . as if you have been having . . . a bloody good time. Bright eyes. Pink cheeks. Mind you, it wouldn't hurt the primary adviser to shave twice a day. (*Smiles reflectively, then a pause as she lets her mind wander back to earlier in the evening. The thought of her diatribe makes*

her do something as extreme as banging herself on the head.) Why did I have to lay all that on him? He was just a nice man and he thought I was interesting, and he *liked* me. And I sit there swigging his wine and going on like . . . and then after all that, he rallies round and gives me the most imaginative, considerate . . . Oh British Leland, you don't advertise these cars at *all* in the right way. Oh, Rose. This isn't going to bring the revolution any close, is it? Well, yes, it *is*. In a way. Every car parked up a lane can be a blow for freedom. So to speak. No, honest, comrade. I would, I really would leave him if it wasn't for the kids. Yes, I suppose I could go and live in a woman's commune. But what if they all turned out to be like Malpass and Smale? All migranes and organising—I couldn't bloody stand it. Well yes, I could get a little house and move in with my mother and kids. She'd love that—built-in baby-sitter, a solid base from which to sally forth as I work my way through the talent at the town. "Rose, your'e never going out on a night like this without your wooly underwear on?" Sally would have us, village school, cider in the afternoons, Geoff would come and see us, practice drinking with Jake. He'd be fine with me out of the way. He doesn't want to be mucky with me anymore, he wants nice clean young secretaries, sort out their critical paths, crack them from first principles. I bet he's lovely with them, he'd be fine, old Geoff, he'd cope . . . Oh, hark at her! "It's a familiar syndrome, Pearson, we see a lot of it round here. To put it simply, a bottle of wine and a bit of unexpected sex drives the poor creatures barmy." (*A sound Off. She freezes.*) Who's that? Alex? Is that you? (*She's quite worried.*) Geoffrey? Geoff, Geoff?
(GEOFF *comes in his dressing gown, he has a bowl of something and a teaspoon.*)

(*With relief.*) Oh, it's you. I thought you were still out. I couldn't think what it was on the top floor.

(GEOFFREY *goes and sits on the bed.*)

What were you doing on the top floor?

GEOFFREY. I couldn't sleep. I went up to the playroom.

ROSE. What for?

GEOFFREY. I don't know. I was eating this.

ROSE. What is it?

GEOFFREY. (*Taking a spoonful.*) It's cocoa mixed up with icing sugar and tinned cream. (*He takes another spoonful.*)

ROSE. What on earth are you eating that for?

GEOFFREY. Because I bloody felt like it!

(*She watches him scrape the bowl.*)

I used to make this for myself when I was a kid. When my parents went out.

ROSE. Are you feeling all right?

GEOFFREY. No, I feel bloody terrible.

ROSE. Oh, lousy evening, was it?

GEOFFREY. I always have a lousy evening.

ROSE. You don't.

GEOFFREY. Where have you been tonight.

ROSE. A meeting. I told you.

GEOFFREY. You're a bloody liar.

ROSE. I am not a liar, I told you it was a meeting, with the primary adviser.

GEOFFREY. Then what did you take your diaphragm for?

ROSE. Why do you do it? You know I hate it, you know it upsets you, so why do you do it?

GEOFFREY. I don't know! It seemed so long waiting for you.

ROSE. You haven't done that for years.

GEOFFREY. How do you know? (*Pause.*) Did you take it?

ROSE. Yes.

GEOFFREY. What for?

ROSE. Just in case!

GEOFFREY. And did you need it?

ROSE. Yes, as it happens. Look stop it, I don't like this.

GEOFFREY. (*Head in hands.*) Oh, Christ. (*Indistinctly into his hands.*) Was it good then? Did you like it? Better than with me?

ROSE. Sorry? What?

GEOFFREY. (*Shouting.*) Was it good, did you like it, better than with me?

ROSE. Well, it was different, you can't compare.

GEOFFREY. How different?

ROSE. Well it was in a car for one thing.

(*Long pause.*)

GEOFFREY. What sort of car?

ROSE. A Maxi. A blue one.

(GEOFFREY *starts to cry.*)

Geoff, oh Geoff don't, please Geoff, don't. I thought you didn't like talking about it, but you know I don't mind, so

GEOFFREY. Can't you see how much you're hurting me?

ROSE. Geoffrey, that's not something I'm doing to hurt you, that's something I'm doing for myself. I'm sorry if you hurt but you're doing the hurting. (*Gently.*) You are responsible for your own feelings.

(GEOFFREY *is crying.*)

Geoffrey! This isn't fair. I thought we agreed to be reasonable, give each other a bit of freedom.

GEOFFREY. I can't keep it up.

ROSE. Oh it's alright for you. You say you're going out for a drink or a meeting, I don't ask any questions about it, do I? I thought the the idea was you'd be the same with me.

GEOFFREY. You want to hear what I do and who I do it with.

ROSE. Only if you want to tell me.

GEOFFREY. All right. When I say I'm going out for a drink, I go out for a drink. By myself.

ROSE. Jesus Christ!

GEOFFREY. And when I say I'm going out for a meeting, I'm going out for a drink. By myself.

ROSE. I don't believe you.

GEOFFREY. I haven't got the energy, to chase 'em any more, I haven't got the energy, I haven't the desire, haven't the need. The last one ditched me in six months ago and it was a relief, it was a bloody relief. So I sit in pubs and drink on my own. When I sense they're starting to talk about me, I switch pubs, but lately I can't seem to get the pints down, and I'm home most nights by ten, wandering round the house crying, banging my head on the bathroom wall . . . looking through your stuff. And . . . There's this new guy at work, Targett, I was talking about him if you were listening. It's a new post. Director of personnel. Well if he's the director of personnel, what does the personnel manager do? I can't tell what I'm supposed to do any more. I go to these meetings, and I can't understand what's going on, because all the decisions have been taken at some other meeting that I don't get invited to, and one of these days I'm going to walk into one of those meetings and it'll be well, Geoffrey, I'm sure you've been feeling as we have that you need to expand your talents in wider fields, the old *chop*, thank you Geoffrey, don't come in Monday. (*He's more or less in tears again.*)

ROSE. I didn't know, Geoff. About work.

GEOFFREY. You care about nothing and you notice bloody nothing!

ROSE. But you're good at your job, Geoff, it's just a rough patch, honest.

GEOFFREY. Targett took that file away from me because he didn't think I was up to it, he doesn't care what I think, I'm not even a bloody threat to him, I tell you, I wake up some mornings scared to go in.

ROSE. Lots of people go through this.

GEOFFREY. I'm not lots of people.

ROSE. No, alright, why don't you have a word with whatisname, you know who I mean. He could get you a month off couldn't he? Give you a chance to sort yourself . . . sort things out. Mm?

GEOFFREY. Sit round the house on my own while you're God knows where, you mean?

ROSE. Oh Geoff I really did think you were having a good time.

GEOFFREY. You've got to give him up. You've got to stop it. I can't cope with it Rose.

ROSE. Geoff, if it's really that that's most important to you. . .

GEOFFREY. Of course it bloody is! I love you! Help me!

ROSE. Oh Geoffrey. (ROSE *drops head, meaning not I love you too darling, but please don't threaten me with that one.*)

(*THE SCHOOL CORRIDOR:* SMALE *comes on as CARETAKER and TEACHERS are moving furniture. As well as necessary scene changes, one might carry across a broken chair, another something smelly wrapped in newspaper.* MALPASS *comes on distressed and weeping.*)

SMALE. (*Very brisk and efficient.*) That's fine Mr. Stokes. . .

STOKES. Like to have five minutes with whoever did this lot, Mrs. Smale.

SMALE. Yes, we're all very upset but I want to be able to ring that bell on the dot of five to nine. (*As he goes.*) Mrs. Malpass! (MALPASS *doesn't respond.*) Beryl. Just go back and check your room before he locks it up, will you?

MALPASS. I don't think . . . I don't think I can go back. When I went in there before . . . I thought I was going to . . . please.

SMALE. Now, Beryl.

MALPASS. My room. All the pictures . . . and the nature table . . . how could anyone do a thing like that? I don't know what I've done to hurt anyone, what have I done to hurt anyone?

SMALE. Oh Beryl, It's not you, it's not personal, they vandalized Mrs. Fidgett's room as well.

MALPASS. But to take the goldfish out of the aquarium and cut then up with scissors. I'm sorry, I know I'm behaving stupidly but. . .

SMALE. Beryl, you've had a terrible shock. You needn't go back to the classroom. But you can cope. You know I rely on you.

ROSE. I've just been in my room, who was it?

SMALE. Ah, good, Mrs. Fidgett, now we only have ten minutes, I want to put your children in with class 4, so if you'd get anything you need from your room. . .

ROSE. Do you know who it was?

SMALE. Vandals, of course, Mrs. Fidgett but that's hardly the point.

ROSE. Well of course it's the point.

SMALE. The children will be here in five minutes, Mrs. Fidgett.

ROSE. Will you stop calling me Mrs. Fidgett and listen! (*Pause.*) We're talking about kids who used to be here.

SMALE. There's absolutely no need to make that assumption.

ROSE. Who else would it be? Have you phoned the police yet?

SMALE. That's all been taken care of. You need not concern yourself about that.

ROSE. But these kids need help, we can't just ignore them. Don't you think that's important?

SMALE. What's important to me is that the children in *this school now* should not be damaged by this—that's fine Mr. Stokes, there's no need for anyone except the staff to know anything about it at all. I shall call Mr. Atkinson at the office now and nothing will get back to the parents.

ROSE. You're trying to pretend that it hasn't happened, but it has! This is what they think of us! It's important!

MALPASS. My children love me!

ROSE. Look. Some kids must have hated so much what happened to them here that they did the worst thing they could of, they came back and chopped up the poor goldfish. Did we do that to them? Do we make them feel like that?

MALPASS. That's a disgraceful thing to say.

SMALE. And a dangerously misguided thing to say. The trouble as I see it is that too many children give the idea that they can think and say and do *anything they like*. And we have seen the results of that. Chopped up goldfish and excrement on the walls! I'm sorry Beryl.

(MALPASS *reacts with a weak "Oh" and runs off.* SMALE *ignores it. Really weighing into* ROSE.)

You haven't been called to any interviews, have you Mrs. Fidgett?

ROSE. Strong! No I haven't.

SMALE. I am not at all surprised. Because before I could give you a good confidential reference, I shall expect to see a steady and continuous improvement in standards on your part, with particular attention to arithmetic, letter formation, discipline, and social training! (SMALE *stalks off.*)

(*Pause.* ROSE *turns to the audience.*)

ROSE. Hands on heads! Fingers on lips! Table six, I'm talking to you. Yes, I'm being strict. Rights, hands down. Show me your clocks. Other way up, *Fraser*.

Now let me see the little hand pointing to the twelve. That's straight up. Point your finger to the brown wire fastened to the little hand. Now show me the big hand pointing to the three. I'm waiting, Amrik. Good. And what colour is the wire fastened to the big hand? That's right, blue. Point to the blue wire. Good. Very good, everyone. Now you all know how to leg a bomb, and you've all got one to take home. You're not here to ask why, *Fraser*, you're here to do as you're told. Now. Put your bombs carefully in your bags. Well take your sandwich box out if there isn't any room. Good. Very good. You've all done very well. *Chairs on tables*! (*She stops. Maybe shakes her head as if to clear it.*) Silly bugger. Might as well cut up the poor old goldfish. Smash the system. I am the bloody system. (*Goes home*:) Sarah! Alex! I'm home!

(GEOFFREY *at the table.*)

Oh! You're back early!

GEOFFREY. As you see. (*He hasn't got the sack has he?*)

ROSE. Hey. They haven't. . .

GEOFFREY. No. Not as yet. No, I was sitting at a meeting, and it suddenly occurred to me that I'd like to go home. So I got up, walked out, got in the car . . . It was easy.

ROSE. That's it?

GEOFFREY. I don't actually give a bugger about it one way or the other.

ROSE. Are you pissed?

GEOFFREY. Umm. Um . . . have you thought any more about what you said this morning?

ROSE. Just . . . just I still think we ought to separate.

GEOFFREY. Look. Um. Sit down a minute. Been thinking how to put this. Want to get it right, you see.

ROSE. What, Geoff?

GEOFFREY. (*Crosses to F.S. stool R. of counter.*) Well. About half an hour after I got home, Sarah came back from Cindy's.

ROSE. What's the matter with Sarah? (*Alarmed for* SARAH.)

GEOFFREY. Nothing's the matter with her. That's not it. Well, she sat down here with me and started telling me how things had gone at Cindy's, and the various odd ways of the Cindy household . . . and then she branched off into the good and bad points of some of her other friends . . . and what might make her flute teacher so sarcastic. . .

ROSE. What's all this about?

GEOFFREY. D'you think you could just listen please? Anyway. It seemed as if what she wanted was a really good long chat. So I got a bottle out . . . and I sat here drinking and listening, and she sat . . . on the table here, telling me all her stuff. Sitting on the table, with her feet resting on my knees. (*Long pause. What the **hell** is this going to lead up to? What frightful revelation? He seems so intent.*)

ROSE. Look. . .

GEOFFREY. That was all, you see. Except that . . . actually while it was going on, not bloody afterwards, or when it was too late, I was thinking that there was absolutely nothing that I'd rather be doing than what I was doing, and absolutely no one I'd rather be with than the person I was with. D'you see what I mean?

ROSE. Yes.

GEOFFREY. I don't know about you, but that's a bloody rare feeling for me. (*Pause.*) If . . . when you leave me, who did you reckon was going to have the kids?

ROSE. Well I would of course. That's what I thought. Didn't you? I'd manage, people do.

GEOFFREY. Could you manage without them?

ROSE. No.

GEOFFREY. Yeah. Thought I ought to mention it. You see, I'd fight you for them, Rose. And, courts being what they are, the odds are that you'd get them. But I ought to tell you, Rose . . . I won't make it easy for you. I'll use everything Rose . . . Your Primary Advisor . . . back seats of cars. . .

ROSE. Oh Christ.

GEOFFREY. And your colleagues at school would be very interested. . .

ROSE. All right!

GEOFFREY. And your mother. . .

ROSE. Oh, for Christ sake, Geoffrey!

GEOFFREY. And the children, yes. Our children. All that could cause a bit of trauma in a child, wouldn't you say? I'm surprised you want to take the risk, Rose.

ROSE. You wouldn't. You wouldn't do that. I don't believe you. You bastard Geoff. You wouldn't do that to the kids.

GEOFFREY. I'm not doing anything to the kids, you stupid bitch. I'm just telling you the way things are, and what you do about them is up to you.

CHILD. (*Offstage.*) Dad! Dad!

GEOFFREY. (*Looking at watch.*) Well, there's no hurry. (*Pause.*) Excuse me. (*He exits.*)

(*As* GEOFFREY *leaves and the lights fade down to a special on* ROSE *we hear children singing "All Things Bright and Beautiful". As the kitchen clears,* ROSE *moves up stage center and the lights come up.*)

ROSE. OK Class Three, gather round. Come on dinosaurs, let's see your faces. Thank you. Now what day is it today? Rachel? Wednesday, right. And who's going to do the calendar today? All right, Fraser, thank you very much. Now, who's noticed anything new today?

Yes. New paint on the walls. Same as before only cleaner, right. They can't fool you, eh Jason? No, the goldfish haven't come back. Well they can't Rachel, because they're dead, but I've got us two new ones. And we'll have to think up some good names for them. And how to look after them. Right, Amrik, because they can't look after themselves like we can. We're in charge, right? Because listen. When you're grown up, you are going to have to make up your own minds about things. There won't always be a teacher there. And for that you have to practice. Right? OK then, so. . . What are we going to do today?

(*As the lights fade to black we hear the sounds of children swell in volume and then cut abruptly off as the curtain comes in.*)

THE LADY WHO CRIED FOX!!!
(LITTLE THEATRE—COMEDY)
By EDWARD CLINTON

3 men, 2 women—Interior

When a jealous actor who's always on the road, finds out his wife has taken on a young male roommate to meet expenses, the show does not go on. He immediately returns home to find out what's going on. The roommate, an inventor who likes to roller skate, is caught in the middle between a jealous husband and frustrated wife. Eventually, all five of the characters get into the act and the result is just plain fun. ". . . punch and humor . . . a funny play. . . ." —Miami Herald. ". . . clever script . . . intriguing sense of humor coupled with a powerful knack for drama. . . ." —Fort Lauderdale News. ". . . funny, delightful and above all devoid of the off color material so many writers feel is essential. . . ." —Hollywood, Fla. Sun Tattler.

(Royalty, $50-$35.)

NOT WITH MY DAUGHTER
(LITTLE THEATRE—COMEDY)
By JAY CHRISTOPHER

3 men, 3 women—Interior

Will Gray suddenly has a problem. His 18-year-old daughter appears at his "swinging singles" apartment door. It seems Will and his neighbor, Rip Tracy, a velvet-voiced radio Dee Jay have a penchant for juggling girls like antacid tablets. Poor Will has a go-go girl in the living room—with her motor running—and a devoted young lady in the bedroom—but that's o.k. since she loves him. Rip has a girl in his apartment already when Will calls on him to also entertain the go-go girl. Then Will's daughter appears to complicate matters further—not only are explanations in order—but daughter has problems of her own. How it all is resolved will leave the audience limp with laughter. An adult play with not one leering joke. It's all in fun. "Funny? Absolutely." —High Point, N.C. Enterprise. ". . . a laugh riot . . ." —Greensboro, N.C. Daily News. ". . . fast-paced farce with as many laughs as you can handle in one sitting." —Lexington, Ky. Herald.

(Royalty, $50-$25.)

A COMMUNITY OF TWO
JEROME CHODOROV

(All Groups) Comedy
4 Men, 3 Women, Interior

Winner of a Tony Award for "Wonderful Town." Co-author of "My Sister Eileen," "Junior Miss," "Anniversary Waltz." This is a charming off-beat comedy about Alix Carpenter, a fortyish divorcee of one month who has been locked out of her own apartment and is rescued by her thrice-divorced neighbor across the hall, Michael Jardeen. During the course of the two hours in which it takes to play out the events of the evening, we meet Alix's ex-husband, a stuffed shirt from Wall Street, her son, who has run away from prep school with his girl, heading for New Mexico and a commune. Michael's current girl friend, Olga, a lady anthropologist just back from Lapland, and Mr. Greenberg, a philosopher-locksmith. All take part in the hilarious doings during a blizzard that rages outside the building and effects everybody's lives. But most of all, and especially, we get to know the eccentric Michael Jardeen, and the confused and charming Alix Carpenter, who discover that love might easily happen, even on a landing, in the course of a couple of hours of highstress living.

> "Thoroughly delightful comedy."—*St. Louis-Post Dispatch*. "A joy."—*Cleveland Plain Dealer*. "Skillful fun by Jerome Chodorov."—*Toronto Globe Star*.

ROYALTY, $50-$35

ROMAN CONQUEST
JOHN PATRICK

(All Groups) Comedy
One set—3 Women, 6 Men

The romantic love story of two American girls living in the romantic city of Rome in a romantic garret at the foot of the famous Spanish steps. One of the world's richest young women takes her less fortunate girl friend to Italy to hide unknown and escape notoriety while she attempts to discover if she has any talent as an artist—free of position and prestige. Their misadventures with language and people supply a delightful evening of pure entertainment. Remember the movies "Three Coins in the Fountain" and "Love Is A Many Splendored Thing"? This new comedy is in the same vein by the same Pulitzer Prize winning playwright.

ROYALTY, $50-$35